For Richard,
with all good wishes,
Sarry Rockstein
April, 1988

The Three Gardens

Laurence Goldstein

THE THREE GARDENS

Copper Beech Press   1987

Some of these poems first appeared in *The Alternative Review, Ann Arbor Review, December, Literature/Film Quarterly, MSS, Ontario Review, Ploughshares, Poetry* ("Homesick in Los Angeles," copyright © 1985 by the Modern Poetry Association), *SITES,* and *The Southern Review.*

"Reunion in Providence" and "The World Overtaken by Ferns" appeared in *Altamira,* published by Abattoir Editions at the University of Nebraska-Omaha in 1978.

The publication of this book was supported in part by a grant from the Horace H. Rackham Fund, University of Michigan.

Cover photograph by Mutlu Konuk.

Library of Congress Cataloging in Publication Data
Goldstein, Laurence, 1943 -
   The three gardens.

   I. Title.
PS3557.0396T47 1987   811'.54   86-32962
ISBN 0-914278-49-5 (pbk. : alk. paper)

First Edition
Printed in the United States of America

for Michael and Akemi Spivack

CONTENTS

Part I

HOMESICK IN LOS ANGELES

Overnight storms have unsmogged the mountains.
I can see their half-million dollar homes
rising like pantheons from the greener scrub.
Here in the basin iceplant gleams under eucalyptus
and bird of paradise so vibrant it seems to take wing.
For this twilight the city should become a single eye
observing its own lucent, lost perfection.

Cyclops waits indoors. My parents sleepwatch
as I tiptoe through the fluent chatter
of some latest Zsa Zsa, avoid her emerald eyes,
the dizzying abyss of her décolletage.
Everyone must see her new picture, she says,
a high-speed chase and numerous fornications.
Unnoticed, I begin to eavesdrop,
and how can the gaze not rest on her smile?

Use has more force than reason.
A Super Chief carried them from Iowa to these shores,
journey I reenacted with toy engines
while they called the stations from Boone to L.A.
Every mile swallowed into this cave of light,
gone with orange groves they tasted of in January
and the facade of Tara pointing toward the sea.

Moistened by rain, pink blossoms glisten
between fingers of the jade tree they planted.
It is brighter inside than the glow of any tree.
News briefs, reruns that kill an hour or two,
then game shows, a movie, and later news.
Every four minutes merchandise bullies them.
Mother and father, how shall I wield my love
against the raucous cannibal of this house?

IN VENICE WEST

. . . it is always 1959.
Minors learn out of school
how to tan their skin as history darkens,
gentle the sun's power with oil
as oil dries up in universal drought.
A Michigan winter's icicle
still embedded in my brain
I strolled the May boardwalk:
bongo drums throbbing a daylong
carotid beat, flutes pumping
their hectic breath in perfect time.

An armistice precedes hostilities,
a space, like this one, for walking
the planks of more pagan days.
The Ice Age will surely come
and the nuclear claw, but not before
this bluegrass group finishes
When My Blue Moon Turns T'Gold Again
or this pierrot extracts a dollar
for his calligraphic broadside:
"This night I followed the unusual glitter of the mist
And saw the lunar priestess close the machine's door.
O Selenite! in this argent climate bide, while rust
Overgrows iron and steel, and makes of the dynamo
Sarcophagus and hoarstone, her monument
Who regathers her robes of silver in the eastern sky!"

The poet was fey and slightly stooped.
He confessed to having Shelley's soul,
his yearning for warm weather, boats,
eccentric company, and early death.
I wished him all of these, and turned
pensively to the Rose Avenue bandshell
where "A Corpse on a Tree" was being mimed.

First the corpse, pancake-white and
weeping, mixed with children in the crowd,
kissing them farewell; then on stage
the invisible noose pulled him tight;
he gasped, gestured a mute appeal
as his heels lifted from the floor.
Some people clapped; some were grave.
Myself, I laughed until the next
Ice Age's memento mori
shifted painfully in my skull.

O what was it like, the unfallen world
before our planet slumped into winter?
Was it like this latter-day Nile,
this prolific, sun-inseminating
Cleopatra's empery of the West?
At noon I did as the natives,
instinctively drifted toward water
where lithe as grunion all ages
frolicked as one, awaiting the rise of
the irresistibly perfect wave.

PALM SPRINGS

It takes your breath away, doesn't it?
The blush of sunset on snow-capped mountains —
that's why I scheduled our visit for this hour.
They say that realtors don't have souls. I do!
If I lived in this safe and beautiful condo
(notice how the butterscotch and cream decor
takes the rosy light — O it's exquisite!),
if I dwelt behind these Bermuda shutters
I would grow younger in spirit every day,
and younger in body, too, as you both will.

How could you not? With the services of
the Nautilus Exercise Room, and golf —
see, you have fairway exposure here —
and a whirlpool spa, and horse corrals. . .
I mean, this place is the fountain of youth.
First your muscle tone will improve.
It's a surprise what muscles come back to life!
Fat just melts away, until you have
proportions like those gods and goddesses
at the Racket Club. Seeing is believing!

I looked up *retire* in the dictionary.
It's from the French, *draw back,* a retreat.
And isn't there so much to retreat from?
I slogged it out, just like you did,
a lifetime — *seven* lifetimes! — in L.A.
No air conditioning for me, no amenities,
no relief from a grinding, dog-eat-dog
upholstery business, and no gratitude
from the kids, either the boy or the girl.
You can bet we looked forward to retirement!

These turnkey condos are *so* nice.
A walled security gate out front, and
look how those fragrant japonica hedges
screen you off from prying eyes.
Just the two of you in this perfect place,
growing younger every day. They call it
Partytown, but I call it Paradise.
You know that *everyone* wants to live here,
those poor souls in Desert Hot Springs,
all parched land and no pest control,

Twenty-Nine Palms with its tacky motels,
Riverside full of Mexicans and smog —
and L.A., that god-forsaken anthill,
ask them in L.A. if they'd like to retire
and languish under these cathedral ceilings
and stroll through our progressive nursery
and take croissants in the atrium any time. . .
Listen, I'm not saying there's no upgrades,
El Dorado was made by people, not God,
but think how many would kill to live here!

Sure, it's expensive. Whatever you stored up,
you'll watch it disappear, but so what?
What's money for if not to buy *just this*,
this shelter from cities, this vista of rose and green?
We tried to make a paradise of our lives
and it turned into L.A. So now
our dreams have a second chance, right here,
not just property that won't depreciate
but heaven on earth. O friends, grab it
before the interest rates go up in March!

INTERVIEW IN A CEILING

What you see of people from this height
isn't very comical. I do get a smile
from the bantams with flashing lights on their shirts
and the shameless girls with no underwear
and blush painted so thick I can see it up here. . .
But those worn-out walking skeletons
heaping side pork and jello in their carts,
it's *them* I have to nail all the time.

Once in a while it's mango chutney or saffron
they tuck into a purse, something fancy
makes them feel high class instead of
what they are — law-abiding poor folk
facing hard times and a marble orchard.
They expect bells to go off, maybe a trapdoor.
What *do* you scare them with? Jail?
Don't make me laugh. Nobody goes to jail anymore.

You remember that cat in the child's book
disappeared except for the smile? Me,
I'm all eyes. I don't exist except
I witness the abuse of so much nourishment.
After hours of staring, the merchandise blurs.
I have to dry-wash and blink several times
before *dairy* or *cereals* or *fruit* separate
into thievable shapes I can save from loss.

Just before something under my charge
drops into a coat it seems to glow clearly
like the cry a lifeguard hears at his station;
or sometimes I get a signal by telepathy.
It's a special faculty, a sixth sense —
entering the thief's mind a second before
his hand furtively touches even a cherry.
And then I ring the security guard down below.

It's a satisfaction and it's justice.
I come from Blue Mound, Kansas, a town
so virtuous even the passers-through
never opened an unlocked door to steal,
not in living memory before the year
I traveled west to preach the Good Word.
A bashful man wants a congregation that
feels his power to teach what they are.

You see that old widow in the black shawl —
no concealing her grief, or his absence —
I've been watching her special for months.
See her hand on the peppers, watch how she
almost sneaks them in the "wrong" bag.
She comes close every time. And if she did steal
when we stopped her outside the electric doors
she'd say, "What's fifty cents to the Safeway?"

You think I don't know her? I *am* her.
Both inmates of some converted motel
with a hot plate and a half Frigidaire
and walls you can push a thumb-tack through
and a thrift shop painting of Jesus over the couch.
All day from Long Beach and Burbank and Downey
bikes roar past like a convoy of tanks
to chew up rabbits and topsoil in the hills.

What happens to all of us is reason for tears.
Even so she can't get away with murder,
not if she has to choke down catfood
the rest of her long retirement, every meal.
It's my mission here, to save . . . not food,
I save *the law* from being eaten up,
the only thing worth preserving, for her sake.
You think that's funny. I don't.

Without spies, they'd close the registers,
put bars on the doors till everyone starved.
They told me honestly when they hired me
and you'd better believe I believe.
I hope to die at my post like an old soldier,
sprawled out over this two-way mirror,
and nobody would guess, not the management,
not all the secret shoplifters-at-heart;

I know what they are and how they'd act.
I imagine them now in front of the meats
or with a meal of scallops in their hand,
turning upward toward the decoy mirrors,
too smart to be fooled, but too scared
to let their worst nature run amuck.
I can die happy just dreaming of righteousness,
that widow paying for spices she wanted to steal.

IN THE SAN CLEMENTE HILLS AFTER
THE JONESTOWN MURDERS

After miles of striding I clamber down
through mustard and Russian thistle
to an arroyo bottom unvisited—

I will suppose — by anything on two feet.
Here wild cattle enjoy the freshest grass,
a green river of spears in autumn drought.

And none of it resurrection of human flesh,
all demi-wilderness east of San Clemente
in its last year or two before sale.

Crimes against nature are news again.
Despite myself I ruminate on them
like a mariner learning of cannibals

or like a Franciscan of Father Serra's time
maddened by the frontier, by hunters
he condemns to burn in the setting sun, forever.

That westering word, *forever*, stone
of strange Temples in the Golden State, seed
more fertile than this migrant tumbleweed. . .

Now I too will sponsor eternal life,
thanks to local atrocities, thanks to
the California light luring the elect.

A pacifist, I have brought to this valley
the first carnage, chased into ambush
that jittery quail the spirit of place.

LONG BEACH

Where I see the marooned Pike
of the Navy's withdrawal,
no longer charismatic tars or hidalgos
casting silver onto the games of chance,
but vagrants who
shuffle by in worn jeans and t-shirts,
stir balloons with badly thrown darts
or heave basketballs to win a pink tiger

she sees the Petrified Man,
his skin bulging with knots,
nearly arboral like the maids of Ovid's book,
greased by sweat from his bald dome down.
"Knock on my leg,
feel the vibration in my skull!"
he exclaimed to a trembling child
who now relives his words with the same salt chill.

She touches my hand. At once
his less-than-ghostly quick
stiffens within me, a source of her craving,
location of sensual undertones
more pungent than
hummingbird stabs of the tattoo
or vomit-smell where the Rotor
turns its barrel of riff-raff at dizzy speed.

In such places I look for
personal history,
the incognitos a wife illuminates,
unlikely grails at the psyche's core.
Two lives have I
so long as I inwardly collect
the resonance of her world,
gather like a bag lady these brittle streets:

First with its fairy-tale goods,
Ocean beyond mother's voice
where under rank boardwalks tongues were given,
Mission of the quavering organ peal,
Oak, site of a
grammar school, where she dunked into
bottomless wells of words
like the unceasing oil pump on Signal Hill.

And so did I drill inward.
I've learned one thing: learning
is more accidental than the order of words,
is a wound the mind reopens by force.
I walk that Pike
like a revenant seeking blood,
a guest in her ruthless Eden
where love for me was made possible by terror.

Part II

THE WORLD OVERTAKEN BY FERNS

It began in the garden.
Mea culpa for extravagant care
and praise more suited to heroes
or blossoms who shake their hips.
These erect backbones of green
repaid watering with no scent,
only the frail, haunting
saw-form of themselves
clinging like rockwool to memory,
standing upright in arctic dreams.

Seedless, they have increased by half.
They sweep at front and back,
washing the porches with their hair.
More than rose and lilac they motion to me,
when I come and go, when I imagine
loveplay, or the final shape of work.

THE THREE MUSKETEERS,
ILLUSTRATED EDITION

Bar Mitzvah was imminent.
Backward you read, and sang
odd pastoral prayers, never
rendered in just the right tone.
When you garbled a phrase, Rabbi
rapped your hand: *golem,* he said.
You added that word to others,
all to be cannonaded from mind
on the second day of manhood,
thirteen and richer than all your tribe.
The ruler slapped at false-elision.
"That hurts." "The world hurts, menchik."

You immersed yourself in Dumas'
high sacramental intrigue,
better than *Bat Boy for the Yankees*
or Tarzan sleeping in the crotch of an oak.
All for one and one for all!
You vaunted that phrase at shul,
struck poses like a Hollywood ham:
swordsman, Queen's agent, Chevalier.

In that blue and grey book you found
a painting of juvenile desire:
Milady-to-be hanging from a bough
while Athos the avenger, maddened
by her incriminating fleur-de-lis
glowered upon her half-nakedness.
"She'll ruin no more lives as she did mine,"
he thought, before urging his horse
toward historic rendezvous. . .
No, nothing of ruin exactly,
but what obsession from that moment!
Death in life's last spasm
thrust up her fulgent breasts

more inviting than a senior girl's.
Sinuous tresses thrilled in the wind.
You stared unremittingly, a scholar.

After the fountain pens, the cufflinks,
the twenty-five dollar bonds,
you gave up Torah, no surprise,
but kept *The Three Musketeers*,
lurid primer with its lucent image
of the teen-angel you too had doomed.
Wicked Milady! of course other names
proved worse: Natalie, Rosanne —
these would break your dumb heart
a century's-length of junior high.
In songs you sent them to execution;
in thoughts no engraving could render
you cast them from Eden, cast yourself.

Now open your own, first book.
Summon manhood, if you can,
and count the unlucky favorites
not quite suffocated by lust:
the fey virgin of Edvard Munch,
the Prince's charismatic waif,
the endangered goddess of the silver screen.
In the last "dismembered" poem
some prey curls inside the cave
of Altamira; you stand beside it;
touch the startled rose torso,
feel the heart's fear of touch.
It leaps into the world's wood.
Comrades bonded by love of chase
follow down the undivided path,
all for one and one for all.
The doe finds no refuge, turns.

"Save me this time," she cries,
shying from the uplifted blade,
"Save me for the love of God!"

Poet, man of much learning,
the book is hard, even for you.

REUNION IN PROVIDENCE

I
Aural wizardry enough — the cackling
of wind up and down the clothesline
as if unminded fabrics wanted breath.
Snapping by the porch, camisoles,
fitful shirts and jeans, skinsheaths
more haunted than their undersouls

twitch noisily, then hush. Nothing
but mailboxes bends the perfect line
extending front by front our sometime home
without relief. Thank God for a messenger.
A snowball could strike the low dome
of Byzantine sky locked on the city square.

I go habitual street by street, pacing
on new-cemented snow the straight lines
and right angles of residential math.
Go downtown, where the trip originates
to that station off the walker's path,
a Jacob's ladder to ethereal states

and my stewardess wife. O the facing
of white one-dimensional lines!
The eye aches for depth; blank ears
attend even the minor slush of boots.
Here is landscape cruel as Lear's —
glacial city that numbs and persecutes.

II
The limo from downtown
shifts up, shifts down
in red-brick sea
of rotted masonry
Main Street behind us
suburbs instantaneous
where Howard Johnson
holds his dominion
Warwick's ruined mill
prison astride the hill
where dormitories run
the interrupted sun
oil derrick aslant
pipe and tubing plant
boxcars of chemical waste
a Pepsi girl defaced
snow fields poles
soft shoulder holes
Turn off — ahead
the airport is spread
space without mass
altitude and glass
Turn off — the limousine
rolls in at T.F. Green.

III
Patience. The wide circles I pace
enlarge like the waiting of centuries.
The echo comes first, the Boeing drone
gathering inmates to runway windows;
we stare intently south, then west.
Our imaginings of joy outdistance
the speed of jets; the gates bend
as the plane takes form.

                Descending
in mimicry of angels the carrier
draws us, one body, to the lap of prayer.
Land safely, Mystery!

                Descending
the wheels reach for earth, and touch.

She descends with the swiftness of sound
still electric on her arms and face,
red hair shaking the light of Asia
out on the Providence breeze.
And then she drifts by real magic in
to hubbub, her cloudy stare poised
while this earthly terminal lays
halo and glare in her blue eyes.
The distances narrow, but they stay,
antipodes I take into my arms.

PREPOSSESSION

Among my projects is an inventory of things
seen only once. Nothing from Ripley,
no anomaly or miracle,

I mean the ghostly life each moment brings,
as when a brunette with jade earrings emerges
from a mock chalet. Never seen before, never,

but in the acid of recollection she and I
dissolve into primal forms of our desire,
familiar as movie stars of the golden age.

She cannot be put into my inventory, neither
unique nor so well known she is only herself.
She must become the shape of her strange original.

Memory is the Stone which makes lead from gold,
as in the haunted bowl the same brunette
now smiles from my childhood, evergreen,

now glides from her fake castle with no future,
vexing passersby as an eidolon of their dreams,
a phantom ship each will board and become its wheel.

I want to see a world newly possessed,
as if angels numerous as the grasses they enter
could shine in the eye's field until it shuts,

as if you, my dear, singular glass that catches
all glints of being, were not only yourself
but the half-sister of apparitions, and their soul.

REUNION AT 35

Here you are, old friend, spelunking
where time's cave bends
toward a perfect century
almost within our fathers' reach.
Is there a single person we revere
who would not hate this age, you ask,
hate it to the death, ours, if he could?
Rash spoilers of our earthly bower,
what termites we are! in damp corners
where Jefferson can't dry us up
or Melville squash us with a book.

Some gassy truths burn like the sun,
never extinguished and never proven.
If you pursue me with light, friend,
I'll grab you inside the cave's mouth
and say, Recollect, come to your senses.
Here is the wood where we tested
one old saw after another, where
in brown uniforms with marching songs
we blazed the paths we know best
and learned to place sticky fingers
on the green wild jasper of life.

Our eleventh spring needs remembering —
that wide marsh in Griffith's wood,
a half-thawed channel crossing
the narrows of its hourglass form.
The troop of us broad-jumped
onto the spongy crust, each leaping
and trampolining till it cracked,
then more gaily cantering on seams
which hissed as our boots landed hard.
Who cared that corneas of dogwood
peered through sycamore like creatures aroused?

Last over the channel, the Scoutmaster
waded slowly through pools of moss.
Go ahead — tear up the place, he said,
if you have to destroy to be happy. . .
Remember how we bridled at that?
As if our ecstasy would stop
the seasonal curdling of the marsh
or turn rivers into it like a dam.
Next year we played and he scolded the same,
his advice more inflexible than the earth
which trembled under us again, but held.

A LETTER TO ANDREW AND JONATHAN

I
Mystery of parentage! The stuffing
    of so many canards
    you're fated to
feel with, as Oedipus or Oliver Twist
when life's vexing feedback
makes you knock at houses never to be your own.
    "Were you ever poor?" asked Emily Dickinson.
    "I *have* been a Beggar."
They say the needy who seek door to door
signify the angels who have never sinned.
    So will you, my adopted boys,
    dearly engrafted as we are,
feast on your occult names,
nourishment of such spice
it chokes up tears on the way down.

II
From the author of this letter
allusions come as no surprise;
here they are remedies not ornaments,
pharmacons, potent self-erasures
when exposure quickens self-disgust.
They will guide you through the mirror
into any neighborhood an author names;
then you are changelings, ragged anonyms,
hero or maiden whose blood
flows when the soul of the action
says, *Advance, perform your desire!*
In such intrigue, my sons,
your father has multiplied
the rich stone of his name,
leaving behind a foreign shape
for unruly rides in stolen cars,
having nothing that is *not* stolen,
not begged or prised away,
in those hours you slept
and midnight waited to close his eyes.

III
Someday, one, then the other of you
while on a forest walk, eyeful
of May apples or skeleton buds,
empty of destination,
will say for the first time,
"Who am I?"
The woods will have their hard answer:
A self is a moment's peace
with the loam you kick as you walk
until it adopts you wholly.
Nature, great maker of nobodies:
"This child I to myself will take"
is all the philosophy it knows.
Gourmet and feast at once,
this green world greedy of life
drinks the blood and the name
with the practiced art of four million years.

IV
Warning: no personal grace
can quell your nemeses, the snobs.
Blood is the wound always on their lips.
Some you will know by the bend-sinister
in their lowered, purebred voices.
These can list the royal family of Liechtenstein.
These have sewn a coat-of-arms on every sweater.
Genealogy is their holy book,
their blind and ambush;
they wade from the marsh elders
pot-shotting with the plosive charge,
their one sanguinary word.
Others are not so absurd, not
Ferraras who say their damages aloud
but acquaintances, even intimates
who share your work and your deserts.
They too seek the mysterious *me*,
rooting day-to-day for favors
only chips off the old block
would claim as rightfully theirs,
theirs not yours, these self-possessed
imply in the manner of a friend.

V
You see, the subject takes us deep.
In whodunits, every suspect is probed
and each is less a suspect
than a phantom who suffers
the searchers' anxiety to reveal.
And two especially, not just guiltless
but blessed in the art of life,
romancers fugitive as the secrets they share,
will seem your familiar embodiment:
surely authors know best why they begin,
and what their unfinished stories are. . .
Who can tell you the unthinkable,
that no *real* parents, no *true* self
wait for your friendly cuffs.
A free assortment of strange lives,
an autumn of falling names
fill up the hollows in our being.
Bygone America fixed "the line of election
through the loins of godly parents."
Our plot is wayward, our age
banquets with aliens to make them brothers.
    So now you have a clue.
    One is all you need.

VI
(While writing, I pause to remember
writing in the small hours, your cradles —
cornucopias of beads, bird-mobiles
and talismans of artificial fur —
halfway between my study and the moon.
In mid-verse an unmuffled cry
would transport me, nourishment in hand.
"Savage is he who saves himself" —
saves by letting himself be nurtured,
a hidden instinct human as words.
Lawless infants, your mother and I
wondered the night away, watching
your full-bellied smiles, enigmas,
miraculous facts fate put in our needy arms.)

VII

From the first, you adopted shapes,
a phalanstery of appetites you named
father, mother, more than friends.
These guardians you parent
will answer more suasively
than writ of blood, or
all the unopened stories
made for you to make your own,
the conundrum of origins.
The imposter seeks to possess,
or be possessed, as if ancestral ghosts
ward off the hauntings they in fact perform.
Better to address the presences
who will be the primal memories you require.
Andrew and Jonathan, in this poem
you will read if you read no other,
your father offers, not alms exactly,
a few resolute words, a charm
in a summer of heart's ease
and your first quizzical *why*'s and *how*'s
on the relations of love.

July-August 1984

Part III

ANN ARBOR SOLITARY

Brawling in the bush with himself
our schnapps-bloated German
punches free to the sidewalk,
mock-orange blossoms in both fists.
His bright yellow blazer, a sign
of bad conscience — for we know
his taste is good, and bottomless —
turns every human head.
It's twilight, his only happy hour.

New faculty have made Germantown
a ghetto of sorts, him a survivor.
He once let drop that my house
havened a devotee of the Führer
who carpentered for the old families.
I imagine these compatriots in song —
swelling the *Horst Wessel Lied*, and
chiming steins at The Heidelberg.

Having nothing on these blocks
to remember, I remember a ghost
who safeguarded the pine floors
and surely gazed with pleasure upon
the celtic patterns of the woodwork,
the chalet-style gingerbread,
the Nordic newel post and moldings
he mined with coverage of the Last Days
when he repaired what I re-repair.

Often I fancy a bull shape
snorting like my sodden neighbor's,
a distemper passionate as his,
eager to trespass and reclaim,
their voices mingled into one
that calls to my boys at catch

across the battlement of spirea,
"Here was a piece of the Fatherland."

46

VERTIGO, A SEQUEL

When Alfred Hitchcock traveled underground
And settled his famous bulk in Charon's boat
("A star vehicle at last!"), and heard the sound
Of oars, and felt the deathship float,

He turned for one last framing glance
At the cool blondes, the shapely auburn-haired,
Whose shades whirled about him in a bawdy dance,
Lifting their crimson dresses, bosoms bared.

His fingers trembled toward Grace
Who modeled once more the postures of sin.
He read the brazen line on her painted face:
"I don't like cold things touching my skin."

He would kill her, again, for saying that.
Strangle or stab, in living room and shower. . .
Hell swung into view like a Hollywood matte;
Kim and Tippi spun beyond his power.

At the helm, some likeness of their leading men
Directed his freight toward the *paysage triste,*
But their king-sized genius, scissors in hand,
Gazed backward till their movement ceased.

RACE AGAINST TIME

Suddenly out from a mariposa screen
Runner seizes the right of way, her lean

sweating legs, and chic sportswear
bouncing before Driver's outraged stare.

Unwillingly brake jerks to floor,
tires squeal, horn utters a roar.

Runner will not yield the single lane.
Driver slows as if heavy rain

or Highway Patrol enforced the law.
How this piece of history sticks in his craw,

that *he* with errands of commerce and world-shaking
wish to further civilize, making

more high-rising mansions of wealth,
suffers postponement while Jane Health

unmechanized treads aimlessly in front,
moving target taunting him with her stunt.

Driver accelerates; his prey looks back
at autos jammed on the asphalt track,

at big rigs with gasoline and food
stalled in first as she makes good

her vow to be an emblem of the lost
animal joy Detroit burned to exhaust.

Almost a mile's frieze fills the road.
Driver honks a warning; the sharp goad

stings; the forked creature prudently flees
the bumper's near-impact for the trees,

turning just in time for Driver's obscene
sign, repeated from every passing machine.

A FILM REVIEW IN THE FORM OF A POEM

"Drive your cart and your plow over the bones of the dead."
A wise ruthless proverb, but no match for nostalgia.
On Hollywood Boulevard bones never stop our progress;
we congregate over star-shaped names of shadows
summoned at the revival house, NuArt or Encore.
And at the Chinese Theatre hands inset into cement
still abide the reverent claspings of pilgrims.
Even a reviewer on routine assignment can be moved
with a seizure of piety for immoderate glamor,
the *elixir vitae* of every filmgoer's days.
Who in this place would call me mad if I sought out
Merle Oberon and easing my palms into hers felt a grasp
like Cathy Earnshaw's cold grip of a more passionate world?

As a child I loved the hand-hammered gold leaf
and hand-woven carpet of the Chinese Theatre,
prayed like the thief of Baghdad that by miracle
I could vault toward Asia to beard Fu Manchu.
And yet *be* Fu Manchu also, Jewish yellow peril,
mastermind, ultimate power of the universe, *Superman!*
How that red-caped muscular titan usurped my God!
My lips intoned the manna-like prose of comic books,
syntax of a city boy for whom *The Daily Planet*
glowed with unsullied virtue like the American past.
And here I am, Clark Kent with no redeeming underwear,
Narcissus in horn-rims, revisitant of oriental camp.
O reader, I was born to review this preposterous film!

What is *Superman* about? One subject only,
the desire to rise into the air by human strength.
Star Wars confused this with hot rods in space,
an impure mixture never my own archaic dream.
Like one of those boys commanded by a Renaissance prince
to flap weighted arms hour after hour, year after year
until his pectoral muscles hardened and he could fly,

I waited for the irresistible impulse to break free,
by downstrokes soar to a rarefied place, and hover.
So I understood Lois Lane's ecstasy in this movie's best scene
when the comic-strip struts of plot were pulled away
and she became airborne on the support of a superhuman arm,
to *be* in flight the secret she had wanted as mere news.
What is cinema for if not to suspend us in such hope?

And plummet downward in horrifying fall!
The wit of Lois's rescue prompted applause,
not so that other violation of common sense,
the lewd farce of Superman's near-fatal drowning.
Kryptonite is no laughing matter, is the gravity
of human nature, green danger of origins, inescapable.
Think how much better *The Man Who Fell to Earth*
expressed the star-orphan's bondage to his doomed nest.
Krypton is a prophetic planet, its annihilation
in spite of Jor-El's eloquence and craft
a figure — who can doubt it? — of our decease.
Uranium-like gem, kryptonite is no simple
Achilles heel of the otherwise perfect Paul Bunyan
but implacable history, in motion every frame of film.

(Cleveland boys with big dreams, nineteen years old,
what blowup did Jerry Siegel and Joe Shuster foresee?
Every moment I sense your presence in this metropolis,
blind Joe unable to watch your boy outrace a train,
Jerry with a heart crippled by the syndicate's greed.
I who write this ephemeral review, hunting and pecking,
know the fatality of art, the descent into Grub Street.
How much more bitterly the makers of Superman's first words
who bartered bird-selves for $130, then plunged to the depths.)

But I digress. "Back to the movie," I hear you say.
Reader, so many themes distract me from my task.
The obliteration of Krypton is a pretty flash of light
and you will enjoy the incandescent moment when
our hero prevents catastrophe along the San Andreas fault
which threatens Hollywood itself with untimely ruin.
And you get the happy ending you desire.
Yes, it's only a movie. You'll forgive me
if I have been unnerved by the dissolution of limits
even in movies, the change of matter into terrifying force.
Earthquakes, fire, flood, ravages of apocalypse;
humans dismembered in slow, *slow* motion;
psychos plunge their knives, fountains of gore
pool in small minds like madness from stroke.
Why do people see such films? I have no choice.

Homo filmex, endangered by species who act their desire,
take heart from this messianic man of celluloid.
Such movies are Kryptonite which we embrace,
dandies of the post-industrial era,
that we may never grow old in one mirror at least,
never lose power so long as remake and sequel beckon.
A wonderful movie. When I emerged from the Chinese
sunlight spangled the inlaid names of the Boulevard.
I testify here I felt at home with the laws of nature,
reconciled to my addiction, my occupation, and my fate.

MOON LANDING

I
"The eye is the window of the soul"

Open-eyed we have kept a weeklong vigil
beside the messenger from heaven
of nonce images, new immortalities.
Now the waiting for vision is over.
Some creature wades through static,
all sheathing and gingerly motion.
A squint will register for eternity
how it descends the ladder while
every worldly eye
opens its shutter, to receive
into the nascent universal soul
the first footstep, the flashing signal
     LIVE FROM THE MOON

II
What is the science of optics?
In Leonardo's era, no science at all:
a jet of species bridged eye and object,
all power from the germinating eye.
"Believing is seeing," he must have been told.
Yet how could human gaze catch in time
the hawk's acrobatic ascent up the breeze,
abruptly tacking its fan of feathers?
No, the eye has no seminal thrust,
lets in all useful goods, a seamstress
making from patches of light
a many-colored coat like the world.

One sees by making: his handcrafted *uccello*
half-joined on the table, enigma, new
thing none but a genius could suture. . .
For this he had watched swallow and kestrel

watch him steal their motions into
his cane-and-taffeta organ of ascent.
Intangible hearsay of other lives
made no impression, not the burning of Savonarola,
the madness of Borgia, the rout of Lodovico,
nor the footsteps of Columbus in the western isles.

When I close my eyes against the moon
I see a strong, full-bearded magus
stretching animal skin over a newmade wing.
Nothing distracts him from the celestial blue
future he strains to welcome like a son.
As he articulates, the ever-swelling Arno
twists in eddies like mountain winds,
lacelike patterns no camera preserves.

The moon has more people than the Ponte Vecchio.

III
The idea of it is now on the streets.
Midway between the pepper trees, neighbors
who have taken imagery into their souls
gather to point upward, grinning like
the Louvre St. John, as if to say
"We have lived to see wonders!"
"But I don't see no rocket up there,"
one woman utters the very truth.
Seeing has already become believing,
or if not, hurry back to television.
Up there is only birds, in summer twilight
seeming to move sideways across the sky.

IV
The world is full of people who have swallowed the moon,
tasted sympathetically the maria's burning crust
or leapt over it like the astronautical cow.
The moon's magnetic field has disappeared
but have we not like the envious eagle
stared into a deity's fountain of fire?
Man will bathe forever in the memory of that fire.

V
A space suit crawls together till
tensed apart; here we must flex
or be mummied, fertile as we are.
Nothing will come of earth.
In five billion years the sun
will flare out, then freeze us dead.
Sister, we evolve in your model.
Satellite ranges will wash down,
marshes occupy urban beds;
as in Leonardo's drawings of the Deluge
accident and force will close our eyes.

For a while I would take solace from evolution:
Apollo's musical origin as a kindling star;
blast of light, wind of pollen on hydrogen fields,
then, invincibly, greenness overtaking planet three.
I would be grateful for the survival of insects
and the variety of birds able to endure the cold,
grateful for the stubborn rooting of mammals
while monstrous lizards went their famished way,
grateful for the teamwork of murderous hunters
and the finger-painted magic oxen of Altamira.
I would applaud the bridging of good and evil by Daedalus.
I would endorse the yearning for flying machines
to sail through the hundred billion stars of our galaxy.

VI
I know sleep will not come tonight.
Prodigal fact peals in every living cell:
like strafing of bells this presence,
these men suited in the science of gods.
Through a neighbor's window I glimpse
an imageless glow of the same conquest.
Almost I wish to take flight through glass
and like Icarus turning his wings to the sun
enter the white heart of that light.

Ancestor of this mid-century's events,
while you improvise I would step
close and linger, swollen with ghostly speech.
You tasted the hawk's tail as a child
and drew the bird of empire; you foresaw
the aeronautical shapes now landed
at the gates of horn, waiting for release.
May your dreamwork be no Pax Americana
but some new age a nationless painter,
young and starry-eyed, might draw from within,
like your self-portrait of Gabriel at his errand,
raising the sign of irresistible news.

THE THREE GARDENS

I
I walked in the Huntington Gardens, that bower
where the most popular species of rose
are cultured by the noblesse oblige of power.

New Dawn crept up a trellis; Good News,
Peace, Mischief — each clearly named —
sought the eye with care-charming pose.

A great house stood nearby, in which famed
''Blue Boy'' hangs, a pretty bloom
whose native ardor Gainsborough tamed.

Perpetuals within stone walls have room
to show forth inward delicacy;
so handiwork baffles doom

when millionaires like Huntington decree,
a man of cultivation and high caste
who had reason to fear mutability.

What he chose to shelter may outlast
dynamos he sent into the world
and their damage to the brittle past.

I wandered by foxglove curled
into healing quivers of calm,
powdery flags Spring had furled.

Not heeding these scrolls of heart's-balm
passersby gazed upward, one by one,
at *bleu celeste* above the towering palm.

"The vault on high" is no longer heaven-haven
but still the fierce realm of welcome rest
we fly at like Icarus challenging the sun.

Daedalus has bound us all to this quest,
beguiling the greatest magi into the skies;
even Leonardo secretly confessed

in the Notebooks of his desire to rise
by his own strength, an airborne sorcerer
and overwhelm the world's daunted armies.

Against the will of such a "necromancer,"
Leonardo wrote, impeaching his soul,
humanity must yield to force, and cower

at "impetuous storms" until control
of government passes into his hands,
his appetites gratified upon the whole

society of nations suffering his demands.
And how would the Huntington Gardens thrive
when the Pharaonic lord of the air disbands

the rights of man, enslaves all things that live?
What shelter will formal beauty find
when will itself ordains which forms survive?

II
Strolling the wide avenues lined
with miscellaneous greenery of many acres
I tried to fix this destiny in mind,

this holocaust foretold by the makers,
ravages we must endure in decades to come,
billions of coal chips pounded by breakers.

No wonder I entered the Japanese Garden numb
with loathing for Man, incomparable fool
who strikes the angel inside him dumb.

But once beside the goldfish-glinting pool
I relented somewhat, by nature being
unwilling to type Homo sapiens as cruel

or nugatory, more fond of seeing
the art of gardens, the caretaking of verse
as humanity's essential show of meaning.

Watery island in a sea of moss,
the pool cast myself back to my eyes,
soothing the strain of nightmare like a nurse.

Fragrance of dogwood unclenched me, bird cries
from cypress columns raising their holy sign
offered the votive pledge of deities.

At one edge of the intricate stone design
I kneeled to bathe my face in my face
which reassembled near the sun at meridian.

As above, so below; even in this artful place
the cosmos lay upon the earthly mirror,
the garden borrowed the scenery of space.

And space is our escape, one seer
has written in his cult-inspiring guide:
"The opening of a new, high frontier."

Colonies of bold scouts will ride
thousands of miles from a launching site
secure as mummies in their pyramid,

waxing on ever-sensible sunlight
louvered through shields to nurture crops.
World beyond world, always in flight,

where the "Hawaiian" temperature never drops,
and strong governments enforce harmony
so that the hive of plenty never stops —

in that immense machine, "Blue Boy"
would find the *vis inertia* that would suffice,
civilization no change would ever destroy.

And it is promised for this great artifice
that rose and foxglove and every other flower
will help restore, in all seasons, our paradise.

III
Spellbound by this vision one hour
as if fixed in place like the ginkgo tree
I thought again of beauty's claim on power,

how Masters bait their line with imagery
culled from pastoral figures of our desire
to involve us in eschatology.

Flatlanders, they say, look higher!
Enter with flying machines the blue void
where blessed spirits dance in the primal fire;

anchor in space or homestead an asteroid;
by sorcery shut down Thanatos!
for as Leonardo's scholar, Freud

wrote in a monograph, it is Eros
we make into the body, motor and wings
of instruments to turn away loss.

But passions made into aerial things —
do they not in history harden
like Almighty whims into thunderings?

Rockets no lunar nymph will pardon
ravage the *agape* of even this manicured
and most innocent Oriental garden.

Now this world of a Creator's measured word
must yield to a tougher kind of nurture:
The Cactus Garden be our symbol of concord.

Huntington made it his prize culture,
the main attraction for all visitors,
who find these forms dreamlike and sinister,

a comic iconography of horrors!
Carnegiea Gigantea, Organ Pipe, Old Man —
these resilient if grotesque reservoirs

through several human lives ripen
on sunlight and far-spreading roots
collecting drops of manna as they can.

I thought, a poet should sing these mutes,
these prickly hosts content with the minimum,
rather than praise his rank above the brutes.

It is time to disown a superlunary emblem,
the aspiration to grow a metal skin
and jet by force of will to kingdom come.

He should praise native succulents, green
barrels of salvation the exile knows,
survivors hardy and still flowering.

I stayed to admire these fit imagoes
placed like characters to show my station
between the lowliest pink and the rise of Apollos.